I0520783

God's By My Side Every Moment

By

Melinda Hadley

Contents

God's By Your Side Every Moment

True Stories to Remind You That You're Never Alone

This book is a collection of true stories—real encounters and testimonies of how God showed up in the middle of my everyday life.

Whether I was walking through deep sorrow or receiving unexpected blessings, He was there.

Each story is a reminder that God is still speaking. He's still healing. He's still walking beside us, even when we don't always feel His presence.

If you've ever wondered, Does God see me? — He does.

If you've ever questioned, Does He care? — He does.

These pages are here to remind you: God's by your side every moment.

Dedication

This book is dedicated to my beautiful Mom, Ilma Oates, who is now with the Lord. Mom, your love, prayers, and example of faith have stayed with me all my life. I thank God for you, and I know one day I'll see you again. Until then, I carry you in my heart every step of the way.

Introduction

I never set out to write a book about my life. Honestly, there were seasons I didn't think I'd survive and moments I thought I'd never want to revisit. But looking back now, I see the hand of God in every step, even in the ones that hurt the most.

This is my story. It's not perfect or polished—it's real. It's the journey of a woman who's faced loss, illness, heartbreak, and impossibilities, yet found hope in the middle of it all. It's about the miracles that came when I least expected them, the lessons I learned the hard way, and the ways God showed up in details so personal they could only have been meant for me.

I'm sharing my life not because I've done everything right, but because God has been faithful even when I didn't understand His plan. My prayer is that as you read, you'll see pieces of your own story in mine—and you'll be reminded that no matter what you're facing, you are never alone.

So come with me. Let's walk together through valleys and mountaintops, and watch how God can take a life—messy, broken, and full of twists and turns—and turn it into something beautiful for His glory.

Chapter 1: Searching For Peace

"My grace is sufficient for thee, for my strength is made perfect in weakness." —2 Corinthians 12:9 (KJV)

A Life Forever Changed

Growing up, I didn't know much about religion or God. Church wasn't a regular part of my life—just something I went to a few times as a kid. I didn't take it seriously. At that age, I didn't understand what faith really meant or why it mattered. Life felt simple then.

But everything changed when I became an adult.

One day, I woke up and realized just how much I needed God in my life. My whole world had turned upside down.

I was twenty years old and pregnant. I had no idea what I was going to do. The fear was overwhelming. I was about to become a mother, and nothing in my life felt stable. My relationship with my boyfriend was already on shaky ground, and I knew it wouldn't last. I was still living at home with my mom and four sisters.

Every thought in my mind revolved around one thing: This child is going

7

to depend on me, and I have to grow up fast.

The Depth of Grief

Despite all the fear and uncertainty, I carried my baby to full term. I went through labor and delivered my baby boy on time. But something was wrong.

In the delivery room, I kept asking, "Where's my baby?" They didn't give him to me right away. I didn't understand why—half an hour passed before a nurse finally walked in holding him. He was beautiful. Perfect. I thought he was just sleeping.

Then she looked at me with tears in her eyes and said she was sorry. My son had died from kidney complications.

The nurse assumed the doctor had already told me. She was bringing him to me not so I could hold him and start our life together, but so I could say goodbye.

I was shattered.

Everything about my pregnancy had seemed normal. The doctor said I was healthy. There were no warnings, no signs that anything was wrong. And yet, I left the hospital days later with empty arms and a broken heart. I didn't even have the strength to attend my own son's funeral. My mother buried him for me.

That pain is hard to put into words.

Numb & Searching

For a long time after, I tried to numb the emptiness. I went out partying. I tried smoking weed. I did anything I could to distract myself or escape the pain, even if just for a moment. But nothing worked. No matter what I did, I kept hitting a brick wall.

I was desperate for peace, but I couldn't find it.

My sister's newborn daughter cried in the next room. Her daughter was born just a month after I lost my son. I had given her everything I bought for him: the clothes, the blankets, the bottles. And every time I heard her baby cry in the night, it echoed inside me like a cruel reminder.

I didn't blame her, but I felt trapped—
surrounded by life, yet carrying death
inside me.

The Breaking Point

One night, the weight became too
much. My heart was already tired, but
now even my body gave up. I had an
asthma attack alone in my room. I
knew what would happen if I didn't
take my medicine—I knew it could
kill me. And in that moment, I wanted
it to. I was done fighting. I didn't want
to feel the pain anymore.

So, I let go.

Somewhere in the middle of the night,
my sister found me. I was
unconscious. She and my mother
rushed me to the hospital. I don't

11

remember the ride. But I remember what happened next.

A Glimpse Beyond This World

I was lying in a hospital bed, and I could hear voices—but I couldn't respond. I was trapped in my own body. The doctor was calling my name, nurses moving around me, machines beeping in chaos—but I couldn't move, couldn't speak. It was terrifying.

Then everything shifted.

My Spirit slipped out of my body, and I floated above myself. I could see them working on me, calling out, trying to revive me. But I wasn't there. I was somewhere else—watching. Weightless.

Suddenly, I started rising. I went up, higher than the hospital walls, higher than the city, into a place that felt endless.

Then the falling started. Fast, hard, terrifying. I plummeted into darkness—thick, hollow, endless darkness. No light. No warmth. Just fear. And I knew: I was heading to a place I didn't want to go.

I wasn't dreaming—I was leaving. Dying. And then, in the middle of that terrifying fall, I remembered something someone once told me: There's power in the name of Jesus.

So I did the only thing I could do—I screamed His name.

"Jesus!" I cried from the core of my being. "Please! I changed my mind. I don't want to die. I want to live, save me!"

Encounter with Jesus

And He came.

I didn't see His face, but I felt Him. Everything stopped. The falling stopped. The fear stopped. His presence surrounded me like light, like safety, like love so deep I couldn't describe it even now.

And I heard Him speak—clear, strong, and calm:

"It's not your time yet. I'm going to take you back."

In a flash, it was like everything went into rewind. My Spirit rushed back down, into the hospital room, into my body, and my eyes flew open.

The doctors couldn't believe it. I had come back. That night, they admitted me to the ICU to watch me closely. But I knew something had already happened—something no machine or medication could measure.

I had encountered the living God.

A New Beginning

That same night, while I lay in that hospital bed, tears rolled down my face. Not from fear anymore—but from the overwhelming presence of God. I couldn't stop crying.

And then, I heard His voice again. Not out loud, but in a still, small voice—so clearly I will never forget it:

"If you don't like your life, give it to Me. Your father died when you were young—let Me Father you. Anything you need, come to Me. I'll take care of you."

At that moment, I surrendered.

I didn't know how to pray. I didn't even know how to repent. But I knew this: I was tired of carrying my pain alone. I hated the life I was living, and if Jesus could give me peace—real peace—I wanted it.

Right there in that hospital bed, I gave my life to Him. I said yes. Yes to His love. Yes to His healing. Yes to a new beginning. And when I did, something happened inside me. Peace—real, pure peace—flooded my soul like a wave.

It was nothing short of a miracle. I didn't see Him with my eyes, but I felt Him so strongly, I knew I would never be the same. When I walked out of that hospital, I walked out a new woman.

I didn't just survive—I began to live.

But the journey wasn't over. What came next would surprise me...

Reflective Thought

Sometimes it takes hitting rock bottom to realize we were never meant to carry the weight of life alone. God often meets us in our most desperate moments—not to condemn us, but to call us back to life.

Takeaway

Jesus doesn't just rescue us from death—He offers us a brand-new life. When we surrender, even without the perfect words, He responds with love, healing, and purpose.

Scripture Focus

"The Lord is close to the brokenhearted and saves those who are crushed in spirit." — Psalm 34:18

"Lord my God, I called to you for help, and you healed me." — Psalm 30:2

Personal Challenge

Reflect on a time when you felt like giving up. What did God teach you in that moment? Consider writing a short letter to Him today—thanking Him for bringing you through.

Prayer

Jesus, thank You for stepping into my darkest night and giving me another chance. I give You my life again today. Teach me how to live in Your peace and not my pain. Amen.

Journaling:

Chapter 2: Life After The Hospital

"But if not, be it known unto thee, O king, that we will not serve thy gods…" —Daniel 3:18 (KJV)

A New Outlook

After I was released from the hospital, everything felt… different. It's hard to explain, but I started to sense that I was becoming someone new—a version of myself I had never known before. It was like meeting me for the first time.

I remember thinking how the grass looked greener, and the sky seemed bluer. I wasn't high—I hadn't smoked anything—but I felt light. Joyful. Like something had truly shifted inside me.

That was all God.

A Changed Heart

Before my encounter with the Lord, I used to cuss like it was second nature. But after accepting Jesus into my heart? Every time I tried, it felt strange, as if I was no longer supposed to be doing it.

I even felt guilty for stepping on an ant. That's when I knew something real was happening, God was changing me.

23

Not just a little, but from the inside out.

Looking back, that was the moment God truly became my Father. He wasn't just someone I'd heard about in church. He was personal. He was real. And He was with me.

A Voice in the Sky

A few weeks later, I joined a Pentecostal church. I didn't know much about church culture, but I was all in.

One Sunday after service, I sat on my porch, deep in thought about everything that had happened and how far I'd come. I looked up at the sky, overwhelmed with gratitude for how good God had been to me.

And then something incredible happened. As I was staring into the sky, I heard a voice say, "Lo, I am with you always, even unto the end of the world."

I blinked, wiped my eyes, and looked again, like, *Did that just happen?* The sky looked normal, but I knew what I heard.

Weeks later, while reading my Bible, I came across that exact same verse in Matthew 28:20. My jaw dropped. That's when I knew for sure—it was God speaking to me that day.

He was reminding me I wasn't alone. Not then. Not now. Not ever.

Reflective Thought

God doesn't just save us—He transforms us. When He enters your life, the world looks different, because your heart has changed.

Takeaway

Spiritual change is more than behavior—it's becoming a new creation. God replaces old patterns with new desires, and His presence stays with us as we learn to walk in our new identity.

Scripture Focus

"Lo, I am with you always, even unto the end of the world." — Matthew 28:20 (KJV)

Personal Challenge

Think about one area of your life where you've seen God changing you. Celebrate that growth—and if you're still waiting for change, invite Him into that space today.

Prayer

God, thank You for staying with me
through every step of transformation.
Keep making me new. Help me see
You in the ordinary, and remind me
I'm never alone. Amen.

Journaling:

Chapter 3: When The Word Comes Alive

"Blessed is the man who trusts in the Lord, whose hope is the Lord." — *Jeremiah 17:7 (KJV)*

Eyes That See, Ears That Hear

One of the most beautiful things I've learned on this journey is that God doesn't just speak through dreams, visions, or voices in the sky—He speaks through His Word. And when He does, it's not just reading—it's like breathing. The words leap off the page and go straight to your heart.

I'll never forget the day I read **Matthew 13:16:**

"Blessed are your eyes, because they see; and your ears, because they hear."

That verse hit me deep. It felt personal—like God was saying, "You're not numb anymore. You can finally see Me, hear Me, and feel Me."

Up until then, life had often felt like a fog. But now, everything around me has new meaning. It was as though scales fell from my eyes. I saw peace in still moments, joy in little things, and the quiet ways God was putting me back together.

His Word was healing me from the inside out.

A Heart Healed at the Altar

Not long after that, I went to a revival night at church. The Presence of God was in the sanctuary. People were expectant—hungry for God.

The guest speaker stepped forward and said something that struck like lightning:

"God wants to heal broken hearts tonight."

Right then, I knew—he was talking to me.

It had been a couple of years since I lost my baby, and though I'd learned to carry on, the grief never really left. I had moved on with life, but the weight of sorrow still lived quietly in the corners of my heart.

So I lifted my hands, barely whispering, "God, I'm ready." In that holy moment, something powerful happened. It felt like God reached into my soul and gently lifted the grief off my chest. The deep ache—the sharp, lingering pain—was gone.

I still missed my son. I always will. But that moment of surrender brought peace I hadn't known was possible. It didn't erase the memory…It just took the sting out of it.

Reflective Thought

There's nothing like the moment when the Bible speaks directly to your heart. That's how you know God's Word isn't just history—it's alive and personal.

Takeaway

The Bible has the power to heal wounds we've hidden for years. When we slow down, open our hearts, and truly listen, God meets us in the silence with words that restore.

Scripture Focus

"Blessed are your eyes, because they see; and your ears, because they hear." — Matthew 13:16

Personal Challenge

Pick one Scripture that stands out to
you. Read it slowly, out loud, and ask
God what He wants you to hear in it
today. Sit quietly with it for a few
minutes and listen. Let it settle into
your heart.

Prayer

Lord, thank You for making Your
Word come alive. Speak to me through
the Scriptures. Heal the places in my
heart that I've kept hidden, and help
me trust You with them. Amen.

Journaling:

Chapter 4: I Got A New Walk

Acts 3:8 (KJV) – "And he leaping up stood, and walked, and entered with them into the temple, walking, and leaping, and praising God."

A Pigeon-Toed Problem

Growing up, my pigeon-toed walk wasn't just a little quirk—it was a source of shame. Boys would whistle or make crude comments as I passed by. As a teen, I tried dance lessons—I took jazz and tap, but ballet was impossible. I couldn't even do a plié

38

with my feet turned out. People pitied me for the way I walked, and often, I just wanted to disappear from the teasing and stares.

As an adult with a decent job and insurance, I finally saw a podiatrist. I was hoping for surgery, but he said the only real solution would have been corrective surgery done as an infant. At my age, nothing could be done. I was too old, and my bones were set.

Walking out of that office, I felt hopeless. I looked up and told my Heavenly Father, "That was my last option. Now what?"

A Surprise Reunion

Two weeks later, I ran into an old acquaintance I hadn't seen in years.

39

She was bubbly and carefree. I couldn't wait to share my testimony with her. Before I could share my story, she told me she, too, had become a Christian. We laughed and hugged, and within the hour, she invited me to her church for the final night of a revival. I was unsure at first because I didn't know what to expect, but I went anyway.

We drove ten miles outside the city to a small storefront church. When we arrived, it wasn't a revival after all— plans had changed. Instead, a few people were gathered in a prayer meeting, standing in a circle and praying over photographs. It felt a little odd. I almost turned to leave. But a whisper in my Spirit gave me peace, saying :

"There are many members in one body."

That Scripture from 1 Corinthians 12 reminded me that God's family isn't one-size-fits-all. We may function differently, but as long as our direction comes from the Head—Jesus Christ— it's okay. So I stayed.

When Faith Meets Feet

After the prayer ended, the pastor greeted me and asked if he could pray for my legs. He said one leg was longer than the other. It sounded strange, but I told him he could.

He asked me to sit in a straight-back chair and stretch out my legs. Sure enough, one leg was visibly shorter. In my mind, I thought, *Really, I never noticed it.*

"Do you believe God can lengthen your legs and make them even?" he asked.

"For me to believe in Jesus was already a miracle," I replied. "He can do anything."

The room grew still as they prayed. At first—nothing. Then I felt a stretch deep inside my leg. It reminded me of how I pulled my Barbie doll's hair to make it longer. I watched in awe as the shorter leg grew painlessly until it matched the other.

I screamed in excitement.

The others watched calmly, as if they had seen miracles like this before. The pastor asked me to stand. I felt different, stable. Then he told me the ground I was standing on was holy and asked me to remove my boots.

Inside my boots, my feet felt light—
aligned. Taking them off, I looked
down and gasped: my toes pointed
straight ahead.

He told me to try a plié.

I bent my knees and turned my feet
outward—and for the first time ever,
my body cooperated. After years of
wanting to dance ballet classes, I was
doing a plié.

We all praised God together. I hugged
my friend and thanked her for inviting
me. That night, I didn't just walk
out—I floated out, completely in awe
of what God had done.

Proof & Mystery

That night, I rushed to my mom's house, eager to show her. She stared at my feet in disbelief, shaking her head in awe. No cast. No crutches. Just two healed feet, walking on their own. She rejoiced with me.

The next morning, I drove a friend back to the building where it had happened—but it was empty. A "For Lease" sign hung on the door. The church I had entered the night before had vanished without a trace.

I tried calling the woman who had taken me there, but she never answered. From the night she dropped me off, I never heard from her again.

Was it the work of an angel? I don't know for sure. But I do know what I heard so clearly in my heart that night:

"I am your God, and you are My people." (KJV) — Jeremiah 30:22

Walking in New Shoes

Still stunned—by the church that disappeared and the friend who vanished—one verse kept echoing in my mind:

"Do not neglect to show hospitality to strangers, for by this some have entertained angels unawares." (KJV) — Hebrews 13:2

That's when I realized: God had sent someone—maybe even an angel—to lead me to my miracle. My faith skyrocketed. I began to understand that walking with God isn't limited to Sundays or prayer meetings. It's about trusting Him with every step, every choice, in every moment.

I asked God, "Did You really do all that just for me?"

And in the quiet of my spirit, I heard His answer:

"I am God. I don't have to ask anyone for permission. I can set up what I want to set up, and I can take down what I want to take down—because I am God, all by Myself."

(KJV) Jeremiah 32:27 " Behold, I am the Lord, the God of all flesh: is there anything too hard for me?"

He reminded me of what He spoke to me back in the hospital:

"Anything you need, come to Me."
Hebrews 4:16(KJV) "Let us therefore
come boldly unto the throne of grace,
that we may obtain mercy, and find
grace to help in time of need."

Today, I still marvel when I walk. My
feet tell a story—not just of healing,
but of divine love. Of a God who cares
about every part of me. Who realigned
bones and rewrote my story.

I walk differently now—not just in
body, but in spirit. My steps are no
longer powered solely by muscle.
They're powered by faith.

Reflective Thought:

Have you ever experienced a moment
that felt beyond explanation—like a

47

divine encounter or a mystery only God could orchestrate? How did it shape your faith?

Takeaway:

God often works in ways we don't fully understand. His power and love transcend human logic. Trusting Him means walking by faith, embracing the mystery, and believing He's working—even when we can't see it.

Scripture Focus:

"Trust in the Lord with all your heart and lean not on your own understanding; in all your ways submit to Him, and He will make your paths straight." — Proverbs 3:5–6 (NIV)

Personal Challenge:

Think back on your life. Can you
identify one moment that felt
undeniably orchestrated by God?
Write it down. Reflect on how it
shaped your faith. Then, thank God for
His mysterious and miraculous
ways—and ask Him to open your eyes
to His work in your life today.

Prayer:

Lord, thank You for being the God of
the impossible. Thank You for
showing up in ways that amaze me and
strengthen my trust in You. Help me to
lean on You, especially when I don't
understand the "how." Remind me that
You are always near, always working,

and always loving me—even in the
mystery. In Jesus' name, amen.

Journaling:

Chapter 5: A Strange Nudge & A Book Purchase

Psalm 144:1 (KJV) – "Blessed be the Lord my strength, which teacheth my hands to war, and my fingers to fight."

A Nudge I Couldn't Ignore

One Sunday before service started, I clearly heard a voice whisper in my ear —not once, not twice, but three times: "Get the book, The Joy of Signing." I looked behind me each time, but no one was there. After service, I went straight to the bookstore, and wouldn't you know it— they had the book. I remember thinking, Sign language? I don't even know anyone who's deaf! But I bought it anyway. I didn't need to understand—God had spoken.

When I got home, I asked Him, "Why this book?" And just as clearly as before, I felt Him answer: "Because I'm anointing your hands to sign."

Stepping Into Something New

I didn't waste time. I started learning the alphabet right away. Day by day, my fingers grew stronger and more fluent. Then one Sunday, I felt God nudge me again: "While the pastor preaches, sign what he says."

There were no deaf people in the room—just a few folks watching me sideways, some chuckling—but I didn't let it stop me.

I remembered Noah. People probably thought he looked crazy, too, building an ark with no rain in sight. But when God speaks, obedience matters more than understanding.

A New Dance Partner

Before I knew Jesus, I loved to be in dance contests in the clubs. But then the Lord told me, "Now I want the glory from your dancing." So I gave it back to Him.

When I'd witness in parking lots or on street corners, I'd break into worship with lip-sync, sign language, and dance. People would stop and stare—but more importantly, some deaf individuals would come up afterward and sign how deeply the music had moved them. I could barely understand them, but I knew God was doing something through those moments.

Vision of Hope

Later, the Lord placed it on my heart to start a dance and sign language ministry for inner-city kids. We called it Vision of Hope. These were kids who had been overlooked, pushed aside, or told they wouldn't amount to much.

With my pastor's support, we set some boundaries: If you weren't respecting authority or doing your best in school, you couldn't minister. We weren't playing around.

Soon, we had over fifty kids. I'd wake up with songs in my Spirit and teach them movements God had shown me. We ministered everywhere—churches, prisons, schools—even internationally, in the Virgin Islands and the Bahamas. And every time someone complimented the kids on how well they performed, they'd smile and say, "We're not performing. We're ministering."

We weren't fluent in sign language, but somehow the deaf understood. God made sure the message got through.

The Fruit of Obedience

Out of those fifty kids, nearly all of them went on to college. Nurses, teachers, business professionals, and even one who became a sign language interpreter. I remember the Lord telling me, "Not one of them will be lost or stray from My presence." My job was to plant the seeds. He would do the rest—and He is faithful.

There was one song in particular—"No Greater Love." That song became our anthem. It reminded us why we did what we did. Not for applause, not for attention—but because of the love of Jesus Christ.

Sometimes I wonder: What if I'd ignored that little whisper in church? What if I'd been too embarrassed to

sign in front of others? I think of all
the lives that would've been missed.

God doesn't need us on a big stage—
He just needs our "yes."

Your Turn to Say Yes

Maybe what God is asking of you feels
strange or uncomfortable. Maybe
you've already counted yourself out.
But I'm telling you—He's not finished
with you. If you've still got breath,
you've still got purpose.

You don't need a perfect plan. Just
take the next step. One "yes" can
change the course of your life—and
someone else's, too.

Reflective Thought

Has God ever asked you to do something that didn't make sense to anyone else? What's stopping you from saying yes?

Takeaway

Obedience might look small at first, but it can lead to something big. God can use your willingness to bless people for generations.

Scripture Focus

**"By faith Noah, when warned about things not yet seen, in holy fear built an ark to save his family." —
Hebrews 11:7 (NIV)**

Personal Challenge:

Ask God to show you one small thing
He's asking of you. Don't wait for
everything to make sense—just say
yes and trust Him with the rest.

Prayer:

Lord, I want to be faithful, even when
I don't understand. Give me the
courage to follow Your voice and say
yes, no matter how small it seems. Use
my obedience to bless others and bring
You glory. In Jesus' name, amen.

Journaling:

Chapter 6: Entertaining Angels Unaware

"Forget not to show love unto strangers: for thereby some have entertained angels unawares." — Hebrews 13:2 (ASV)

A Conversation in Sign

Some years after I'd started learning sign language on my own, I decided to take a beginner's class to grow more confident. Our teacher was deaf, and one evening I asked her how to sign the word heaven. She showed me, and

I signed back, asking, "Do you want to go there?" She shrugged, like, *I hope so*. Right there in class, I signed to her about Jesus—how He saved me, and that she could know Him too.

After class, as I was leaving, a woman stopped me in the hallway. She said, "I couldn't help but notice your conversation with the teacher... can you tell me more about Jesus?" So we stood there and talked for about twenty minutes—just me, sharing what God had done in my life.

While we were talking, I noticed a man standing nearby. He didn't say a word, just stood there with his arms folded, smiling and nodding like he was enjoying every word. At one point, I said to her, "I don't want to keep your friend waiting," and pointed

65

at him. She turned to look and said,
"He's not with me."

We looked back—and he was gone.
Where he was standing, he would've
had to walk past us to leave, but we
never saw him move.

Heaven Paid My Bill

The next day, I came home with a
friend and grabbed the mail. I told her
how I was only able to pay $50 on
my electric bill that month—it had
climbed into the hundreds—and said,
"I just hope they don't cut me off."

Holding my breath, I opened the new
bill… and it said I only owed $50. I
stared at it, confused. "No way," I said.

I called the electric company and told them there must've been a mistake. The woman on the phone was blunt: "There's no mistake," she said. "Just pay the $50 when you can." Then she hung up!

My friend looked at me wide-eyed and said, "I wish that could happen to me!"

That night, I sat with both bills in my hands—old and new—stunned. Then I heard the Lord speak to my Spirit: "That was Me last night at your school, watching you share about Me. I smiled. And it was I who erased your bill. Because you take care of my business, I'm taking care of yours."

That man wasn't just some bystander—he was an angel.

The McDonald's Mystery

After I'd joined the usher board at
church, one of my duties was helping
visitors find seats. One Sunday, the
church was especially full, and a
woman stopped me and asked what
time the service would end. Then she
asked if she could use a phone to call
her job and say she'd be a little late. I
led her through the basement and up to
the pastor's office.

She said she worked at a McDonald's
on the Northside and needed to check
in with her manager. After the service,
she thanked me and said she'd really
enjoyed it.

A few days later, I happened to be on
that side of town and felt nudged to
stop by the McDonald's. I asked about
her, gave a description, and the

manager said, "No one by that description has ever worked here." I walked out of there dumbfounded.

Later that evening, while I was praying, the Lord answered what I hadn't even spoken yet: "She was an angel. I wanted to see how My people would treat Me if I walked into My own church. You did well."

A Man on the Curb

It was a hot Sunday, and I arrived at church early, but left to pick up my friend's son. On my way, I saw two little girls walking and struggling with their bags. I stopped and gave them a ride. As I turned onto their street, I noticed a man sitting alone on the curb. He looked tired, possibly homeless.

I dropped the girls off, then saw the man again on my way back. This time, I slowed down and said something to him. I told him I didn't give men rides, but I gave him directions and invited him to church. He said he'd try to come.

After the service, I remembered him and told a deacon the story. I described what he looked like. The deacon looked surprised and said, "That man was here. He sat on the balcony the entire time." I felt chills.

Later that week, while praying for him, the Lord spoke gently to my Spirit:

"That man was an angel in disguise. Many passed by him that morning, hurrying to get to My house. They passed Me by. But you didn't. You invited Me in. Thank you."

Reflective Thought

Have you ever had a moment that felt too perfectly timed—or too strange—to just be a coincidence? What if those moments are Heaven checking in, seeing how we treat people God sends our way?

Takeaway

God pays attention to how we treat strangers, especially when we think no one is watching. Angels don't always come with wings or halos. Sometimes they're sitting on the curb, smiling in

71

the hallway, or asking to borrow a
phone. When we take care of God's
business—by showing love, slowing
down, and being obedient—He takes
care of ours. You never know when
you're entertaining angels unaware.

Scripture Focus

**"Be not forgetful to entertain
strangers: for thereby some have
entertained angels unawares." —
Hebrews 13:2 (KJV)**

Personal Challenge

Be intentional this week about how
you treat those who seem overlooked,
different, or in need. Ask God to help

72

you see people through His eyes—and stay open to the idea that someone you serve may not be just anyone.

Prayer:

Lord, thank You for reminding me that You show up in the everyday moments—sometimes through people I'd never expect. Help me not to miss You. Teach me to slow down, be kind, and love without needing a reason. Make me alert to divine appointments and willing to respond in love. I want to take care of what matters to You. Amen.

Journaling:

Chapter 7:
Selah Moment –
Listen With
Your Heart

Take a breath. This is a space to pause.
Maybe God is trying to say something
quiet but powerful. Listen with your
heart.

"To what can I compare this
generation? They are like children
sitting in the marketplaces and calling
out to others: 'We played the pipe for
you, and you did not dance; we sang a

dirge, and you did not mourn.'" —
Matthew 11:16-17 (NIV)

This verse stopped me one day. It's
Jesus talking, and He's basically
saying: "No matter how I came, you
didn't respond." That really hit me.

John the Baptist came fasting and
praying—people said he was too
much. Jesus came healing, eating with
people, showing love—and they still
criticized. It didn't matter how God
showed up… their hearts weren't open.

Sometimes we do that too. We want
God to speak loudly. But sometimes
He's gentle. Sometimes He dances and
wants us to join in. Other times, He
mourns and calls us to sit with Him
quietly. But do we even notice? Are
we so caught up in what we expect
that we miss what He's actually doing?

This is your invitation: don't miss Him.

Reflective Thought

Have I been so focused on what I want to hear that I've ignored what God's actually saying?

Takeaway

God speaks in many ways—through joy, through sorrow, through silence, and through strangers. We just have to stay open.

Scripture Focus

"Whoever has ears, let them hear."
— Matthew 11:15 (NIV)

Personal Challenge

Take a quiet moment today. No distractions. Ask the Lord, "What have You been trying to say that I haven't heard?" Be still. Listen. Write it down.

Prayer

Lord, forgive me for the times I've tuned You out. I don't want to miss a single thing You're doing. Help me hear You in the loud moments and the quiet ones. Let my heart stay soft and ready. I'm listening. In Jesus' name, amen.

Journaling: Have You Entertained an Angel?

Prompt: Think back—was there ever a moment you felt a stranger might have been sent by God? What did you do? What would you do now?

Chapter 8: Shut the Door

"And we know that in all things God works for the good of those who love Him…" — Romans 8:28 (NIV)

A New Year, A Sudden Decline

The new year had just begun, and already my body was failing me. I couldn't move like I used to—my arms and legs felt heavy, unresponsive. My feet burned with pain, like I was walking on nails.

I rushed to the ER, but the tests came back normal—no heart attack. No

stroke. Still, something wasn't right.
They told me to follow up with my
primary doctor. When I did, he took
one look and said he was sure it was
spinal stenosis. He'd seen it before and
immediately scheduled scans and
began discussing treatment.

I left his office with fear gripping my
heart. Sitting in my car, the tears came
fast. I didn't know what this diagnosis
meant for me. All I could feel was
dread.

Turning Panic Into Praise

But something shifted by the time I got
home. I chose not to live in fear.
Instead of letting despair take over, I
walked inside, shut the door, and got

before the Lord. I didn't wait to feel
better—I praised through the pain.

I told the Lord, "No matter what
happens, I will praise You. I trust that
somehow, some way, this is going to
work out for my good."

Even when it hurt to lie down or get
out of bed, I reminded myself: we
don't fight for victory—we fight from
it. Jesus already won. That truth
became my anchor.

A Morning Miracle

Two days later, I woke up—and
something was different. No pain. I
stood up. I lifted my arms. I kicked my
legs. I walked the house praising God.
He had healed me, in my sleep.

I still went through with the CT scans, and the results confirmed what I already knew: my spine looked perfect. The doctors and nurses were amazed. Just days before, I'd barely been able to move. Now I was wearing heels, climbing stairs, and moving like I never had an issue at all.

God had restored me completely—not just physically, but spiritually, too. My faith had grown stronger in the storm.

More Than I Asked For

That same week, while getting ready for bed, I heard God whisper, "Check your upper thigh." For months, I'd had a rash there—something the doctor said might never go away.

But when I checked, it was gone. The Lord spoke to my heart: "When I healed your arms and legs, I healed that too."

God didn't just fix the obvious issue— He went above and beyond. That's just how He works. When He heals, He makes us whole.

Reflective Thought

When unexpected trials hit, do you let fear set the tone—or do you take time to shut the door and invite God into your situation? What could shift if your first instinct was worship, not worry?

Takeaway

There is power in shutting the door on fear and opening your heart to faith. When we respond with praise, we position ourselves to witness God's power. Victory isn't always instant, but peace comes the moment we surrender. God is faithful—even in the silence, even in the waiting.

Scripture Focus

"You will keep in perfect peace those whose minds are steadfast, because they trust in you." — Isaiah 26:3 (NIV)

Personal Challenge

This week, when fear or pain creeps
in, take time to "shut the door."
Whether that means turning off
distractions or finding a quiet space,
go to God first. Praise Him in advance.
Declare His promises over your life.
Watch what He does when you give
Him your full attention.

Prayer

Lord, in every trial, remind me to shut
the door and make room for You.
When fear rises, help me respond with
faith. I thank You that healing, peace,
and victory are mine in Christ. I
choose to worship You before the
answer comes, because You are
worthy always. In Jesus' name, amen.

Journaling:

Chapter 9: He Left... But God Stayed

"And we know that in all things God works for the good of those who love Him..." — Romans 8:28 (NIV)

The Fight Was Spiritual

I always dreamed of marriage, imagining I'd feel like Cinderella. I thought I was ready when the one I prayed for came—but life had a different plan. Addiction quietly took hold, and one day, he was gone.

91

We were married 18 years—years of hopes, struggles, laughs, and tears. I prayed, fasted, and fought for our marriage. Yet despite my efforts, I had to face a loss I never imagined.

When He Left

When he left, my world fell apart. I felt rejected, abandoned, and alone. Eighteen years ended—not with a neat goodbye, but with sorrow and brokenness.

But God? He didn't leave. Even in my tears and self-doubt, He stayed. He whispered, "You're still loved. I haven't forgotten you."

The Struggle

The silence was deafening. Explaining what happened meant facing judgment, pity, and advice I didn't ask for. I questioned myself endlessly.

God met me in that mess. He reminded me—He was there. And when it was time to let go, He held me together. I was still His daughter.

God's Quiet Faithfulness

Healing didn't happen overnight. God worked slowly—through a Bible verse, a song on the radio, or a text from someone who didn't even know I needed encouragement.

93

One day, overwhelmed with anger and grief, God asked:

"How can you be mad at someone in the ICU?"

Then He said:

"You're the nurse. How can a nurse be mad at a patient who needs healing? They can't help themselves. If they knew how to love you, they would— but right now, they can't even love themselves."

It hit me hard. I began letting go of the anger—not for him, but for me. Real healing started when I stopped praying for him to come back and prayed for his soul instead. True love wants the best for someone, even if you don't get anything in return.

Lessons Learned:

Healing doesn't always come the way we expect. But God still heals.

When you stay close to Him in the pain, He can do something new.

God redefined me—not as a divorced woman, but as His daughter, deeply loved.

Marriage isn't just companionship. It's ministry—a call to love sacrificially, to pray for someone else's soul, sometimes to lay down what you want so they can live.

I didn't get the love or partnership I prayed for. But I discovered who I was becoming in Christ.

Even when I felt alone, God was working behind the scenes—healing, restoring, building something new.

God also taught me to be careful whose advice I accept. Some haven't healed from their own pain, and their bitterness can seep into your heart.

Now, my life is full of His presence. He's teaching me to forgive—the same way He forgives me. It's not always easy. It's a daily choice. But that's where freedom begins.

Reflective Thought:

God uses what breaks us to build us.
He uses what we lose to show us what
He's forming.

Takeaway:

Marriage is a ministry that changes
you—even when it doesn't go as
planned. Let God work in you,
because who you become reflects
Him.

Scripture Focus:

**"And we all... are being
transformed into his image with**

**ever-increasing glory, which comes from the Lord, who is the Spirit." —
2 Corinthians 3:18 (NIV)**

Personal Challenge:

Ask God what He's teaching you—not about the other person, but about how He's shaping you. Write down one thing He's showing you about your heart and thank Him for not wasting your pain.

Prayer:

Father, thank You for not letting me stay the same. Even through the pain, You're shaping me to look more like

You. Help me see others like You see them—as souls who need grace. Teach me to love like You, even when it's hard. Thank You for turning loss into growth. In Jesus' name, amen.

Journaling:

Chapter 10: Devotional Interlude

You Can Change Your Story & Take Destiny Steps

You may have started out wrong. Maybe life hit you hard right from the beginning. Maybe your foundation was shaky, or somewhere along the way, you lost your footing. Maybe you got stuck in the middle—stuck in pain, regret, fear, or just trying to survive. But listen to me… You still have the power, through Christ, to change your ending. God hasn't changed His mind about you.

He knew every twist and turn your life would take, and He still called you. Still chose you. Still has a purpose for you. Your mistakes don't cancel out your destiny—they just become part of your testimony.

Now is the time to take destiny steps. Not giant leaps, not perfection—just small steps of obedience and faith. A destiny step is praying when you feel empty. It's showing up when you feel unseen. It's trusting God when everything around you says, "give up." It's saying yes even when your knees are shaking.

Each step you take in faith moves you closer to the life God has already prepared for you. Destiny doesn't happen all at once. It's walked out daily—through surrender, through courage, through believing that God's plan is bigger than your past.

So don't let fear keep you frozen. Don't let shame keep you silent. Don't let what happened back then convince you that God can't use you now. What He placed in you is still alive. You were born with purpose. You were born to impact. And you're not too late.

Take the step. Start again. Forgive. Heal. Apply. Launch it. Speak it. Write it. Walk it. Whatever it is—just move. Because when you walk with God, every step is a destiny step. Your story is changing, and your destiny is calling.

Reflective Thought

What's been holding you back from moving forward? Are you stuck in your past, or ready to say yes to the next step?

Takeaway

You can't change how your story started, but with God, you can change how it ends.

Scripture Focus

"Better is the end of a thing than its beginning..."
—Ecclesiastes 7:8 (KJV)

"The steps of a good man are

ordered by the Lord: and he delighteth in his way." —Psalm 37:23 (KJV)

Personal Challenge

This week, ask God to show you one "destiny step" you can take. It might be making a phone call, starting something new, or letting something go. Then do it—no matter how small it feels.

Prayer

Lord, I thank You that my past doesn't define me. Even if I got off to a rough start, You still have a plan for my life. Please give me the courage to take the next step, even when I feel afraid. Remind me that You go before me and walk beside me. Help me trust You with my ending. I'm ready to move forward—in faith, in hope, and purpose. In Jesus' name, amen.

Journaling:

Chapter 11: God Has Gone Before You

"And my God shall supply all your needs according to His riches in glory by Christ Jesus." — Philippians 4:19 (NKJV)

The Whisper

At the end of 2014, the Lord whispered something unusual to me:

"Your next car will be baby blue, have low mileage, and you'll only pay $100 a month."

At the time, it sounded a little far-fetched. I was still driving my Malibu, and it was doing fine. I told a few friends what God had said, and they gave me that look—you know, the one that says, "Alright… sure." I tucked the promise away in my heart and kept moving forward.

Breakdown or Breakthrough?

A few months later, in early 2015, I headed out one Friday morning to have my car checked at the dealership—and it broke down on the way there. I had to have it towed to the

111

shop. Later that evening, I got the call: the Malibu was totaled.

Strangely, I wasn't upset. I told my mom, "Well, I guess I'll just have more time to spend with the Lord now." Since I was retired, I figured this was just another opportunity for quiet time with Him.

A Nudge & A Promise

The next day, my mom suggested, "Why don't you take my car and go look around for something new?"

That made sense… except I didn't have a down payment. Still, I decided it wouldn't hurt to look.

I visited the dealership connected to
my bank and asked to see their
cheapest cars. That's when I heard God
whisper again:

"Don't forget the car I promised you."

It all came rushing back. When the
saleswoman asked me what kind of car
I wanted, I told her, "I want either a
Malibu or a Toyota, but it has to be
baby blue, not have a lot of miles, and
be practically new."

She looked stunned. "You're not going
to believe this… the car you just
described—the exact make, model,
color, and condition—is being
delivered right now—it's on its way
here."

She pulled up a picture on the computer. When I saw it, I knew: that was my car.

Faith Meets Provision

She sent me to the loan officer, and I was approved without any issues. By the time I returned, the car had arrived. I took it for a test drive, and it felt right. I told her, "I'll take it."

Then came the paperwork. The monthly payment was far more than $100.

I paused. "Wait… God said I'd only pay $100 a month."

She smiled gently. "Well, you'll probably need a cheaper car then."

114

I could have settled, but even though it didn't make sense at the time, I knew what God had already told me. I said, "No. I'm sticking with this one. I know what the Lord told me."

She agreed to hold the car until Monday while they cleaned it up.

The Unexpected Answer

The price of the car was far more than what I could handle, but I knew God had told me to get it. After I returned my mom's car to her, I told her everything. She asked, "If I gave you $100 a month, could you cover the rest?" I said yes. Later that night at home, I prayed, "Lord, even with her help, this is still a stretch."

Then the Lord reminded me to call my ex-mother-in-law, because we had just talked earlier that morning. I could tell she had been praying for me before she even spoke. I shared the whole story with her, and she said, "God told me not to help you fix your old car." I told her, "I'm glad you listened to the Lord because there was a lot wrong with my car."

To my surprise, she continued, "But what He did say was to help pay your car note. How much is it?" When I told her, she said, "You just pay $100 a month, and I'll pay the rest."

I burst into tears. I couldn't believe she would do that for me. She and my mom sent the payments faithfully until the car was paid in full. God did exactly what He said—He lined it all up, down to the smallest detail.

Just One More Thing

Right before I picked up the car, I thought, "It would be nice if it had a remote start."

As if on cue, the woman said, "Oh—I forgot to mention—it comes with remote start!"

That Monday, I sat in my driveway with the car and asked the Lord, "Why baby blue? You know my favorite color is red."

He gently replied, "Because blue represents the heavens. I want you to remember—you are always surrounded by Me."

God remembered what I had forgotten. He didn't just provide—He exceeded

117

every expectation. He made it
personal. He made it heavenly.

Reflective Thought:

Have you ever had a moment when
God reminded you, "I haven't
forgotten you"? He knows your needs,
your heart's desires, and even the little
things you don't say out loud.

Takeaway:

God is a provider, yes—but even more
than that, He's your Father. He cares
about every detail. When He gives you
a word, hold on to it. Don't settle. He's
already ahead of you, preparing the
way.

Scripture Focus:

"And my God shall supply all your needs according to His riches in glory by Christ Jesus." — Philippians 4:19 (NKJV)

Personal Challenge:

Think back to a promise God made to you—something you tucked away because it felt too bold or too specific. Bring it back to Him in prayer. Let Him show you how He's been working behind the scenes all along.

Prayer:

Lord,

119

Thank You for being a God who goes before me. You see the big picture, and You care about the smallest details. Forgive me when I doubt or forget what You've said. Help me to trust You deeply—to hold on to Your promises and wait with expectation. You're always working, even when I don't see it. Thank You for loving me that personally.

In Jesus' name, Amen.

Journal Prompt: Reflect & Write: Promises You've Received

Think back to a time when God gave you a promise, a word, or a hint about your future. How did it make you feel at the time?

Journal Prompt: Moments of Provision

Write about a moment when God surprisingly provided for you, especially when it seemed impossible or didn't make sense.

Journal Prompt: Trusting Beyond Understanding

Are there areas in your life where God has asked you to trust Him even when it doesn't make sense? How can you surrender fully to His timing and provision?

Journal Prompt: Gratitude for Details

God cares about the smallest details in your life. List three ways you've seen His personal care or attention to detail recently.

Journal Prompt: Prayer Reflection

Write a short prayer thanking God for going before you and providing for you in ways only He can.

Chapter 12: Praise Him Anyway

"My grace is sufficient for you, for My strength is made perfect in weakness."— 2 Corinthians 12:9 (NKJV)

When God Asked Me to Dance

I never imagined God would call me to dance again in my sixties.

At church, the younger women were preparing a worship dance for an upcoming event. That's when I felt a

131

familiar nudge in my Spirit. The Lord was inviting me to join them.

I laughed to myself—much like Sarah did when she overheard God's promise of a child. "Really, God?" I asked. "You want me to dance?"

What no one knew was that I was struggling just to walk. My body was weak. I couldn't even twist the cap off a water bottle. I relied on a lift chair to get up and a walker to move from room to room.

Yet deep in my Spirit, I knew God was saying,

"You have a part in this."

I cried out,

"Lord, how can I do this? My Spirit is willing, but my flesh is so tired."

132

That's when He gave me this
Scripture:

> "After they were severely beaten,
> they were thrown into prison…
> Paul and Silas, undaunted, prayed
> in the middle of the night and
> sang songs of praise to God…
> Suddenly, a great earthquake
> shook the foundations of the
> prison.
> All at once, every prison door
> flung open and the chains of all
> the prisoners came loose." —
> Acts 16:23 26 (TPT)

Then He whispered:

"Learn how to worship Me in the
midst of your pain. Don't look
around—look up. I've got you."

Dancing on Air

When my feet touched the stage that Saturday, it felt like I was dancing on air. The pain didn't vanish, but God placed His strength on my weakness.

It wasn't performance—it was worship. His Spirit moved through me, carrying what my body couldn't. But as soon as I stepped off the stage, the pain returned. I could barely walk.

Then someone told us we'd been asked to dance again the next day—twice.

"Lord, help…" I whispered.

I was sore and exhausted. Still, God said, "Yes. Do it again."

And He did. He gave me just enough strength, exactly when I needed it.

A Word for You

Let me say this from experience:

When we stay in the Spirit, God will
give us the strength we need—right
when we need it. We won't always
understand why the pain remains. But
we don't walk by explanations—we
walk by faith.

Joy in the Surgery Room

Two days later, another challenge
awaited me: a biopsy to investigate the
cause behind my muscle weakness.
That day, I felt at peace—confident
and free of worry. I was ready to step
in and have it done.

The surgery room felt like a
celebration. There was laughter and

135

peace—even in pre-op. Nurses kept walking in, smiling.

"What's so funny?" they asked.

It was the joy of the Lord. Even in a surgical suite, His presence made itself known. And I remembered Paul's words:

> "In everything give thanks,
> for this is the will of God in
> Christ Jesus concerning you."
> — 1 Thessalonians 5:18 (KJV)

So I'll say it again:

Praise Him anyway.

Praise Him when you can't walk.

Praise Him when it hurts.

Praise Him when it doesn't make sense.

Because praise isn't just what we do after the victory— It's often what brings the chains loose.

Reflective Thought

When life feels heavy and your strength is gone, what's your first response—complaining, withdrawing, or worship?

What might shift in your situation if you chose to praise God in the pain?

Takeaway

God may not always remove the pain—but He meets you in it. Worship through your weakness and invite heaven's strength into your struggle.

Praise is a powerful weapon—not just for victory, but for survival.

Scripture Focus

"My grace is sufficient for you, for My strength is made perfect in weakness." — 2 Corinthians 12:9 (NKJV)

Personal Challenge

Is there something you've avoided because of pain, fear, or fatigue? Ask God to meet you in that space. Take one step of faith.

Your act of worship might be the beginning of your breakthrough.

Prayer

Lord,

I may not have the strength I want, but I trust You will give me what I need.

Help me to praise You, even when it hurts.

Teach me to worship in the valley—
not just on the mountain.

Let Your power be seen in my
weakness.

Use my life as a testimony of Your
strength.

In Jesus' name, Amen.

Journaling:

Melinda Hadley: God's By My Side Ever Moment

Chapter 13: What's Happening Now

2 Corinthians 4:8–9 (KJV) – "We are troubled on every side, yet not distressed; we are perplexed, but not in despair; persecuted, but not forsaken; cast down, but not destroyed."

This year has been a journey I will remember. One test after another, and still nothing definite concerning the loss of my mobility. Then came hernia surgery, back-to-back asthma attacks,

143

and UTIs that hit like waves trying to knock me down.

Physically, I was worn out. But spiritually, I clung to God tighter than ever. I always have to remember that God is with me—and I'm never alone. He's been in every hospital bed, every waiting room, every lonely moment. He still is.

I still press my way to church on Sundays, even when it's hard. I've needed help just getting out of a chair—and the love I've received from my church family has reminded me I'm not in this fight alone.

I worship with lifted hands when my body feels weak, because my spirit is still strong. I smile and encourage others, not to hide my pain, but because I've found purpose in it.

I want healing. I want to walk without a walker again. But until that day comes, I'll worship in the middle of the struggle. He's still worthy. He's still good. And my life still has purpose.

Pain doesn't cancel purpose. Suffering doesn't silence your song. If anything, it makes your praise more powerful.

Reflective Thought:

You don't have to wait for healing to worship. Your most powerful praise might come from your hardest place.

Takeaway:

Even when you feel broken, you're not useless in God's hands. He works powerfully through your weakness.

Scripture Focus:

"My grace is sufficient for thee, for my strength is made perfect in weakness." —2 Corinthians 12:9 (KJV)

Personal Challenge:

Whatever pain you're walking through, bring your worship with you. Choose to glorify God right where you are.

Prayer:

Lord, You see every struggle. Thank You for staying close, even when my body is weak. I trust You for healing, but until it comes, I'll keep praising You. Use my life—even in pain—to show Your glory. In Jesus' name, amen.

Journaling Prompt: What "Still I Rise" moments have you had this year?

Journal Prompt: In what ways has God shown you His presence through physical or emotional trials?

Chapter 14:
Little Niche
Blessings

*Psalm 68:19 (KJV) – "Blessed be
the Lord, who daily loadeth us
with benefits, even the God of our
salvation. Selah."*

Even with everything going on, I made
up my mind: I wasn't going to let
discouragement win. "Even if He
doesn't deliver me today, I still won't
bow."

I wasn't bowing to fear, sickness, or
sadness. I stood in faith and told the

enemy, "You won't get joy out of me doubting my God."

What could've pulled me into depression, I gave to God. What could've filled me with fear, I released in faith. I kept a spirit of gratitude, even while hurting.

And then, I started ministering despite it. Yes, ministering from my hospital bed, ministering in the waiting room, ministering to the nurses and staff. God was using me right where I was.

At home, I told the Lord, "I want to do church ministry, but I can't do it like this." And He responded clearly: "Yes, you can. A pulpit is not just at church, but it's wherever you are. You may not be able to leave the house, but you can pray, you can call and encourage others with your words, and you can

153

still love people right where you are."
Ministry is my life—and it doesn't stop
just because it's uncomfortable.

And God saw me.

One morning, I told God I felt a little
down. Hours later, one of my spiritual
daughters showed up at my door with
a bouquet of roses. She said the Lord
had placed me in her heart, and she
was supposed to come over and bless
me financially. She didn't know why,
but she said she wanted to be obedient
to God. I hadn't told anyone what I
asked God for—only God. He used her
to show me that He hears my every cry
and knows my every thought.

Then a few days later, I told the Lord
how I missed going outside because it
was difficult for me to walk. I said, "I
wish I could just get some fresh air."
And out of nowhere, a sister/ neighbor

from my church called and said, "The Lord told me to bless you with a motorized scooter." Surprisingly, it was my favorite color, red. Nobody but God could have done this. Now I can ride through the neighborhood and breathe in the fresh air again as much as I want.

He saw me. He kept sending signs of His love through people—a reminder that I'm not forgotten.

Reflective Thought:

God doesn't just walk with you—He sends signs along the way to remind you He sees you.

Takeaway:

Faith in the fire opens doors for ministry. And God knows how to reach you personally in the middle of it.

Scripture Focus:

"But if not, be it known unto thee, O king, that we will not serve thy gods…" —Daniel 3:18 (KJV)

Personal Challenge:

Look for the roses. Look for the scooter. Don't miss the signs that God sees you.

156

Prayer:

Lord, thank You for the personal ways
You remind me I'm seen. I won't bow
to fear—I'll stand in faith, trusting that
You know exactly where I am and
what I need. In Jesus' name, amen.

Journaling Prompt: When was the time you felt seen by God in a personal way?

Journal Prompt: How has He reminded you that your life still has purpose—even in pain?

Epilogue: A Letter to My 20-Year-Old Self

Written on 05/21/2021

There are times I wish I could go back and talk to the younger me—not to change anything, but just to offer some hope, some comfort, and a glimpse of how things would turn out. If I could sit next to my 20-year-old self in one of the hardest seasons of my life, this is what I'd say.

Dear Me,

I know it doesn't feel like life has been fair to you. Right now, you're in the thick of something so painful you can barely breathe. You're grieving the loss of your newborn baby boy, and the weight of it is crushing you. The pain feels like it's never going to end, and I know you've started to believe there's no way out. You're even thinking about ending it all.

But I need you to hold on.

You're not losing your mind. You're not too far gone. God is about to step in and rescue you—from the pain, from the despair, even from yourself. He's going to pull you out of this dark place. I know you've always wanted to be a daddy's girl, especially since your father passed before you were even

163

born. What you don't know yet is that your Heavenly Father is about to step in and fill that role in a way you never thought possible.

Your life isn't over. It's just about to begin.

In just a couple of years, you're going to give your life to Jesus—and when you do, He's going to become everything you've been missing. You'll start calling Him "Daddy" because that's how real and close He'll be to you. He's going to heal your broken heart. And the way you see life? It's going to change completely.

What you thought was the end is really the beginning.

That moment when you tried to take your own life—God is going to use even that. You'll have an out-of-body experience in that hospital room, and Jesus will visit you right there in the ICU. That's when the new you will begin to rise. You won't even believe what He's going to do.

He'll heal your pigeon-toed feet faster than you can blink. No one will believe it, but it's real. He'll anoint your hands to learn sign language. Before you know it, you'll be using that gift to bless children and adults alike—people from all over, in ways you can't even imagine right now.

You won't have any more biological children, but don't let that scare you. God's going to bless you with so many spiritual children, you won't be able to count them. You'll nurture, teach, and pour into others in a way that only a spiritual mother can. And yes, it won't be easy. You'll face rejection, you'll face battles—but God's hand will always be on you. He'll protect you from every attack.

You won't walk this journey alone. God will place mentors in your path who will teach you how to draw closer to Him. You'll have favor with God and with people. You'll be amazed at how He uses everything you've been through to bless others and bring Him glory.

You'll look back one day and see how none of it was wasted. So don't give up, baby girl. Your pain is not the end of the story. There's so much purpose ahead. Accepting Christ into your life is the promise that one day you'll see your baby again—whole, smiling, and waiting for you in heaven. But in the meantime, God has life for you to live—real, full, joyful life. You're going to smile again. You're going to

166

laugh again. You're going to see how every broken piece comes together into something beautiful.

Peace is coming. Joy is coming. Healing is coming. Hold on.

Love, the older you

Devotional Reflection

Reflective Thought

What would you say to your younger
self if you could go back and speak
life into them? What pain would you
tell them they'd survive? What beauty
would you show them is waiting on
the other side?

Takeaway

Your past doesn't disqualify you—God
can redeem it all. Every tear, every
loss, every dark place becomes part of
the testimony He writes through your
life. He was there then. He's here now.
And He's already gone ahead of you.

Scripture Focus

"'For I know the plans I have for you,' declares the Lord, 'plans to prosper you and not to harm you, plans to give you a hope and a future.'" —Jeremiah 29:11 (NIV)

Personal Challenge

Take time this week to write a letter to your younger self. Speak from a place of healing, truth, and grace. Then pause and thank God for how far He's brought you—and for the work He's still doing in you.

Prayer

Father, thank You for never giving up on me. Thank You for seeing beyond my pain and into my purpose. I'm so grateful that even when I wanted to give up, You held on to me. Help me to see myself the way You see me— not through the lens of my past, but through the promise of what You're doing in me. Heal the places that still ache, and use my story to give hope to someone else. I trust You with every part of my journey. In Jesus' name, Amen.

Journaling: Letter to My Younger Self

Take a moment to reflect on a time in your life when you felt broken, uncertain, or afraid. What would you say to yourself now, from the perspective of healing and faith?

Dear Younger Me...

Journaling: Looking Ahead with Hope

Write down what you now believe about your future. What is God speaking to your heart about your next season?

Lord, I believe…

About the Author

With a heart full of grace and a life marked by God's miracles, Melinda Hadley shares her personal journey of faith, healing, and transformation through this devotional.

From moments of deep loss and miraculous healing to divine

encounters and unexpected callings, her story points readers back to the faithful presence of God.

She is the founder of Vision of Hope, a ministry devoted to worship through dance and sign language—reaching inner-city youth and the deaf community. Her obedience to God's voice, even when the path was uncertain, has touched countless lives and continues to be a testimony of His power and grace.

Melinda currently resides in Racine, Wisconsin, and lives each day with purpose—choosing faith over fear and trust over doubt. Her prayer is that through this devotional, you'll see how truly present God is—in every moment.

"And we know that in all things
God works for the good of those
who love Him,
who have been called according
to His purpose."
— Romans 8:28 (NIV)